# CONTENTS

In the 1950s, most workers in Britain were men doing tough work with their hands such as mining, ship-building or farming. As these industries went into decline, new jobs were created in services such as banking, shops and tourism. The workplace changed too. More women went to work and new technology, such as computers, required new skills. In 21st-century Britain, few people are working the same way as their grandparents did.

▲ A newly-painted train engine, built in 1948. British industry began to pick up after the war.

## THEN AND NOW

In the past 20 years, the growth of technology, especially the Internet, has transformed the way people work – just think of Internet shopping. In 1988, 50,000 computers were connected to the Internet worldwide. By 2007, the number worldwide had risen to over 1,000 million computers.

## BOOM AND BUST

The 1950s and 60s were a boom period for Britain. Millions of new jobs were created for nurses, teachers and social workers. Every year, from 1953-57, 300,000 new homes were built.

## AFTER THE WAR

At the end of World War II (1939-1945), the British economy was in a mess. The cost of fighting the war had left the government badly in debt. The new Labour government was determined to get everyone back to work. They did not forget the Depression in the early 1930s, when millions of people were unemployed and, as a result, many families lived in poverty. By 1948, the economy started to pick up, helped by a loan from the United States of $3.75 billion.

▲ A car dealer doing a brisk trade in Birmingham during the 1960s.

▲ Many new jobs have appeared in the service industries, such as call centres.

Thousands of immigrants from former colonies in India, Pakistan and the Caribbean were invited to Britain to help rebuild the country. However, though Britain was doing well, it was already struggling to keep up with its major rivals: the United States, Germany and Japan. By the early 1970s, the boom was over. Consumers were buying cheap cars, radios and TVs made in Japan and other overseas markets. Computers did jobs previously done by people. People wanted gas or oil central heating rather than dirty coal fires in their homes. As a result, many British factories and mines closed in the 1980s.

## NEW DIRECTIONS

In the last 20 years, while many "traditional" jobs have been lost, more and more people have been working in services such as banking, IT (information technology) and tourism rather than in factories. Computers and the Internet have helped small businesses to thrive, and many more people work for themselves.

> " *Go around the country, go to the industrial towns, go to the farms and you will see a state of prosperity such as we have never had in my lifetime – nor indeed in the history of this country.* "
>
> Prime Minister Harold Macmillan speaking on 20th July, 1957. But the boom was not to last.

## BUZZ BOX

**The switch from industrial to service jobs has meant that some areas have done better than others. London and Southeast England are better off while the Northeast (steel and shipbuilding), Wales (mining) and Northern Ireland (shipbuilding) have all been badly hit by the decline in industry. From 1997–2000, wages in Northern Ireland were two thirds those in London.**

## TIMELINE

**1948**
The Labour Party creates the Welfare State, which aims to provide health, housing, education and social security "from cradle to grave".

**1950s**
The beginning of economic boom in Britain. The average working wage is £7.28 per week.

**1960s**
The average working wage is £14.10 a week.

**1973**
Miners' strike and oil crisis.

**1980s**
The privatization of state-owned industries by Conservative party. The average working wage is £127.70 a week.

**Late 1990s**
Economic boom.

**2005**
Average working wage is £447 a week.

# INDUSTRIAL WORKERS

Working conditions in factories and coal mines in the 1950s were very different compared with today. In the past, people worked more with their hands than their heads. Modern factory workers use computer controls to operate massive industrial robots – they are expected to think while they work.

## HARD, DIRTY WORK

Fifty years ago, workplaces were often noisy and dirty places. Mill workers in Lancashire had to put up with the crunching wheels of machines, the shriek of steam from the boilers and the constant beat of the looms. People often worked very long hours for low wages. In the 1950s, large gangs of men were employed to do jobs which today would need fewer workers helped by modern machines. Large factories such as the British Motor Corporation car plant in Longbridge, Birmingham employed thousands of workers.

> 66 *We used to walk from Failsworth every day – hail, rain, or shine, to start work at 7.30am, until 5pm, with an hour off for lunch, on your feet the whole time… the canteen trolley used to come around, in the midst of all the cotton fluff, and oil everywhere: it was no wonder there was so much bronchitis about, we were breathing the cotton fluff constantly.* 99

Mavis Revell, a cotton worker at the Asia Mill in Hollinwood, Manchester, in 1957.

▲ Teenage girls at work spinning cotton at the Lily Mill in Shaw, Lancashire, in 1957.

### THEN AND NOW

Coal miners in the late 1940s cut coal by hand using a pick. It was backbreaking work. The men had little protective clothing apart from a hard hat and studded boots. Older miners suffered from silicosis (a lung disease caused by dust) and stooped from bending over all day. Today the work is done by radio-controlled cutting machines. Miners wear a helmet, ear defenders, kneepads, gloves, safety glasses, battery lamp and a self-rescuer, a device that allows them to breathe in the event of an underground fire.

◄ A Yorkshire coal miner at work in 1949.

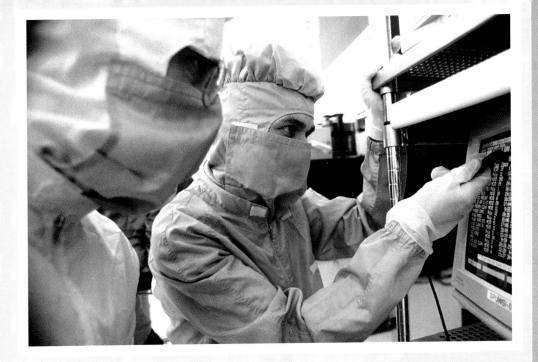

▲ Workers wear protective clothing in a modern electronics factory in Newcastle. Safety is taken very seriously.

## TIMELINE

**1947**
Fuel Crisis due to shortage of labour in coal industry.

**1950s**
There are 690,000 coal miners working in Britain.

**1965**
Service industries employ the bulk of Britain's workers.

**1970**
30 per cent of jobs in manufacturing.

**1975**
North Sea oil starts being pumped ashore.

**1994**
17,000 coal miners in Britain.

**2006**
Just 13 per cent of jobs are in manufacturing.

## KEEPING SAFE

There were often accidents at work, especially in the mines. On 29 May 1951, 81 miners and two rescue workers died after being trapped underground by an explosion in Easington colliery in County Durham. Since the Health and Safety at Work Act 1974, however, working conditions have got a lot better. Today, machines or robots do much of the heavy or dangerous work.

Many modern factories also have better facilities for their workers, such as canteens, medical clinics and sports grounds.

## DECLINE IN MANUFACTURING

After World War II, almost half of all workers in Britain were employed in manufacturing. Up until the 1960s, a job was seen as a job for life. Today, however, only 15 per cent of workers make a living from manufacturing. In the 1960s, when British steel works and mines began to close down, it was hard to get other jobs nearby. Many people were forced to move further and further to find work. In recent years more manufacturing jobs have disappeared as British firms have struggled to compete with overseas rivals paying their workers much lower wages.

## BUZZ BOX

In the 1930s, over a million people worked in the British car industry, producing 500,000 vehicles a year. In 2006, over 1.5 million cars were made in Britain, and the industry employed around 800,000 people, but virtually all of the major car factories were foreign-owned.

Over the past 50 years, farming has become more and more reliant on machinery. Many traditional farm skills have been lost. Today there are far fewer farmers and many farms are run more like factories. However, outbreaks of disease, such as foot-and-mouth, have encouraged some farmers to go back to more traditional, "green" methods.

> *" In the early years the farm was completely worked with horses and around 18 were kept… We had two or three farm workers who lived in, plus another four or five who travelled to work from local villages. We also had casual labourers at busy times, hay making, harvesting and hoeing root crops. They used to sleep out in the buildings and used to come to the back door to collect their food. "*

Dorothy E. Garbutt describes life on a farm in the 1950s in Oswaldkirk in North Yorkshire.

▲ A farmer ploughing the fields using two shire horses in Kent, 1950.

## TRADITIONAL METHODS

In the 1940s and 50s, farm labourers needed to be able to turn their hand to a wide range of tasks such as seed sowing, weeding, mowing, spreading dung and threshing after the harvest. The tools they used were heavy and the jobs tiring. Life was hard and as late as the 1960s, many farm workers lived in tiny cottages without bathrooms or electricity.

Today, farm labourers may spend many hours each day sitting in a tractor. They need to know how to operate a variety of machinery such as muck-spreaders, straw-balers, mowers and forklift trucks.

▲ A popular tractor model dating from the 1950s.

▲ A farmer milking cows in a mechanised milking parlour in Suffolk, 1990.

## THE NEED FOR FOOD

When the war ended, the government encouraged British farmers to produce as much homegrown food as they could. To help farmers achieve this, the Agriculture Act of 1947 provided loans to help them buy labour-saving machines. While this did speed up production, it also meant that many agricultural workers lost their jobs. Between 1945 and 1992, the total number of jobs on English farms fell from 478,000 to 135,000.

## FACTORY FARMING

From the 1950s onwards, farmers were also encouraged to use new types of seeds, fertilisers and pesticides to become more productive. Smaller farms that kept a few pigs and cattle were replaced by factory farms.

## NEW PROBLEMS

In the past decade, outbreaks of disease such as BSE and foot-and mouth have put some shoppers off British meat. Cheap imports and low supermarket prices have also made it very hard to make a living from farming since the 1990s.

THEN AND NOW

In the 1950s, some farmers continued to use horses – this took a lot of strength and skill. In the 1970s, giant machines such as combine harvesters could do the same work in a day it had taken 12 men a week to do 30 years earlier.

**1947**
Agriculture Act provides grants to farmers to buy machinery. This leads to the Meat and Livestock Commission (MLC) in 1967, which aims to modernise farms and increase meat production.

**1970s**
Combine harvesters speed up crop harvesting.

**1973**
Britain joins the European Economic Community (EEC). British farmers get subsidies and grants from the Common Agricultural Policy (CAP).

**1989-1996**
The EEC bans the export of British beef following the BSE scare.

**2001**
Outbreak of foot-and-mouth disease.

**2002**
Strategy for Sustainable Farming and Food provides £500m to encourage "green" farming.

# SHOP WORKERS

Shops in the early 1950s were very different to shops today. There was no self-service and instead of big supermarkets there were lots of smaller shops selling everything from butter to boot polish. Today shopping is dominated by big superstores on the outskirts of town. Supermarket assistants spend their time stacking shelves or working at a till rather than serving individual customers.

▲ Under rationing, you bought items using coupons. If you ran out of coupons, you couldn't buy the item.

## RATIONING

World War II had a big effect on shops. Basic foods such as meat, sugar and butter and clothes were rationed to make sure everyone got a fair share. Shop assistants had to check coupons in the ration book and deal with long queues. Rationing did not end until 1954.

The end of rationing saw a consumer boom and the rise of supermarkets. There was such a rush on goods that in 1954 customers in Birmingham could expect delays of three months for electrical goods, four months for furniture and a year for a new car.

## NO TIME FOR CHAT

In the new supermarkets that appeared from 1948 onwards, people served themselves and paid for goods as they left the shop. Prices were often much cheaper so people stopped going to local shops. Traditional shops, such as bakers, grocers and butchers, began to disappear. The job of shop assistants also changed. In the 1940s, they served customers one at a time. Now they spent most of the day stacking shelves or sitting at a till.

In the 1950s, shop assistants were expected to dress smartly. The staff in large department stores wore black jackets, striped trousers and stiff white collars. Though many shop workers are still expected to wear a uniform, their dress has become a lot more casual.

## BUZZ BOX

In the new supermarkets, wire baskets were used to reduce the risk of shop-lifting and to allow shoppers to select their own goods and carry them to the checkout. Not everyone liked the new baskets – one female shopper is said to have hurled her wire basket at Alan Sainsbury in disgust at the opening of a new Sainsbury's store in the early 1950s.

▲ Traffic-free shopping in Chelmsford, Essex.

## ALL UNDER ONE ROOF

In the past 30 years, many town centres have been closed off to traffic to create shopping precincts. In addition to this, huge indoor shopping centres, copying giant US shopping malls, have grown up on the outskirts of cities. Opening hours have got longer, too. Many superstores are now open on Sundays, which in the past was a day when all shops had to shut by law.

▼ Britain's biggest shopping centre, Bluewater, in Kent.

66 *Shop assistants may have long working hours in this day and age. But at least when it comes to 5 or 6 in the evening they can shut up shop and go home. What about other professions that have to work much longer shifts, very often without the half-hour lunch break shop assistants are entitled to?* 99

Anoo Gupta talking about Asian shops in Manchester.

## TIMELINE

**1940s**
Food is rationed during the war. Most people still shop in local shops.

**1947**
Just ten self-service shops in Britain.

**1948**
The first supermarket opens in Britain.

**1954**
Meat rationing finally ends, nine years after World War II ends. Eggs cost 23 pence per dozen.

**1969**
There are 3,400 supermarkets in Britain.

**1995**
Tesco creates the first supermarket loyalty card scheme.

**2007**
Around 26 million British Internet shoppers spend a total of £42 billion online.

# THE SERVICE INDUSTRY

From the 1950s onwards, a dramatic shift took place in the workforce, sending individuals who had worked in factories, plants and mills into jobs in offices. Today, millions of British workers have jobs in government, banking, IT, entertainment and other services.

## SERVICE JOBS

The service sector has grown rapidly since the end of World War II. The creation of the Welfare State in the late 1940s led to many new jobs in the Health Service and in the Department for Social Security (DFSS), and over the next 50 years other jobs were created in services such as banking, shops and tourism. These jobs needed very different skills from traditional manufacturing jobs.

▲ A group of office workers at their computers.

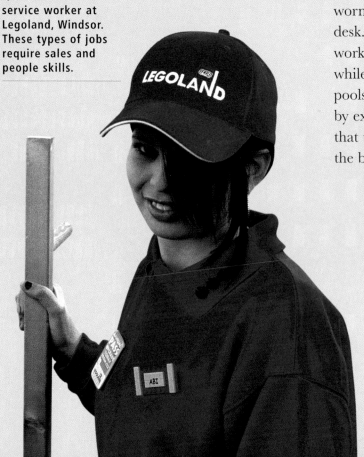

▼ A customer service worker at Legoland, Windsor. These types of jobs require sales and people skills.

## A DAY AT THE OFFICE

Office workers, often called "white-collar workers" because of the standard suit and tie worn in offices, spent much of their time at a desk. Before the arrival of computers, an office worker might spend many hours filing reports while secretaries worked in clattering "typing pools" churning out a stream of letters dictated by executives. Many office workers had time cards that they used to "punch in" or "punch out" at the beginning and end of each day to show the

## BUZZ BOX

In the 1950s, many executives worked in their own office cut off from other workers. The 1960s saw the rise of the "office landscape" – workspaces were organised to help people work more efficiently. Over 30 years later, most white-collar staff work in cubicles in open plan offices.

hours they had worked. However, by the 1960s, offices were already changing. Managers realized that people needed more variety in their jobs to prevent them becoming bored, and as a result, less efficient.

## REVOLUTION IN TECHNOLOGY

In the 1970s the electric typewriter was replaced by word processors, which combined the typewriter keyboard with the brain of a computer. By the 1990s, word processing became just another bit of software in a PC. Fax machines provided a fast way of sending written information overseas. The arrival of the Internet and emails in the 1990s transformed the office once again. Email allowed people on opposite sides of the world to work together on projects and share information as if they were in the same room.

▲ Modern offices have computers that allow us to communicate with people all over the world.

In the 1950s and 1960s, office workers were also expected to dress smartly. In London, bank workers wore bowler hats into work until the early 1970s. However, in the 1970s more fashionable elements crept in and by the 1980s office workers wore shoulder pads, wide lapels and baggy trousers. Today's dress codes are more relaxed and some "white-collar workers" wear jeans to work.

## TIMELINE

**1949**
Bell Telephones introduces the Model 500, the first desk phone.

**1950**
The first Xerox photocopiers roll off the assembly line.

**1950s**
Electric typewriters become common in offices.

**1965**
Cubicle design first appears in open plan offices.

**1971**
The Wang 1200 is the world's first word processor.

**1980s**
Faxes become popular in offices.

**1990s**
Digital telephone systems are used in offices.

**2007**
Smoking is banned in all indoor workplaces.

# THE RISE OF MACHINES

One of the biggest changes in the workplace has been in the use of machines to do unpleasant or dangerous jobs. In the 1950s, many British workers feared mass unemployment as machines took their jobs. So far, though, while new technology has led to job losses in some areas, it has created new jobs elsewhere. Robots tend to do boring, repetitive jobs, while skilled workers who can operate automated machinery remain in demand.

▲ Workers feed coloured yarns on to rollers as they make carpets in a textile factory during the 1950s.

▼ The vast majority of cars in Britain today are made by robots.

## JOB LOSSES

In the 1950s, factories had been using moving belts to create a production line of workers for 30 years. But as time passed, machines did more and more jobs. This allowed many employers to cut down the number of workers. Many lost their jobs in factories and farms in the 1950s and 60s as a result.

## TIRELESS WORKERS

Robots are used to carry out a wide range of tasks, such as welding or spray-painting cars. They can carry out heavy work 24 hours a day, 7 days a week, often in conditions that would be uncomfortable and even dangerous for human workers. The use of automated machinery also cuts down on accidents. Today, all sorts of processes are controlled by computers, such as handling the sacks in a tea processing plant or making electronic circuit boards. The growth of machines means that workers in factories

So far, some jobs have been unchanged by automation. A building site today looks very similar to one 50 years ago – human workers with trowels, saws and hammers building houses. In restaurants, people serve food, sweep the floor and operate the till just as they did in the 1950s.

today are not just needed for muscle. They have to be able to understand machines and the computers that control them.

## COMPUTERS AND THE INTERNET

Offices no longer employ large numbers of typists and filing clerks. These jobs have been replaced by computers. However, new technology also creates new jobs. People need to build, operate and maintain IT systems and a whole new industry has grown up based on this. Computers and the Internet have also changed how firms sell their products. Many have online catalogues from which customers can order products and services. Other websites conduct market research or provide promotional materials, adverts, and other types of information.

66 *The process worker had to become a bloke that knew instruments and how to use instruments because the machinery was geared that way. Machines were getting programmed and things like that.* 99

Arthur Baker, maintenance worker, speaking in 1984.

### BUZZ BOX

Another big change in the 1950s was the switch from coal to electricity in factories. At first this led to job losses in the mining industry, but it also made industrial towns much cleaner, without soot and grime.

▲ Many of us now do our shopping on the Internet, which means companies have changed the type of jobs they offer to cater for this demand.

**1951**
Univac I is the first mass-produced computer.

**1956**
The first telephone cable is laid between Britain and the United States.

**1970**
The first computer mouse goes on sale.

**1984**
The Apple Macintosh computer is launched.

**1985**
Microsoft Windows is launched.

**1986**
Nearly 40 per cent of British workers use computerized or automated equipment.

**1992**
Nearly 60 per cent of British workers use computerized or automated equipment.

In the 21st century, workers can easily put in a gruelling 10-hour work day without ever stepping outside their front door. New technology has also helped many people set up their own businesses and allows busy executives to carry on working while they are travelling on business trips.

▲ A worker at the control panel of an electronic office in 1955. Computers were very rare at that time.

## BUZZ BOX

Some jobs can now be done from anywhere in the world. But this can also lead to job losses in Britain. Many call centres and helplines for British companies are now based in India.

## WORKING FROM HOME

A home office with a computer, a fax machine and a telephone allows workers to communicate with colleagues anywhere in the world. They can send and receive emails and electronic files and can meet through three-way telephone calls or video links. For the employer, having fewer people in the office cuts down on costs. For the home worker, less time spent commuting to work means more time for family and less stress.

## CRAFT WORKERS

In the early 1950s, the only people able to work from home were those employed in small businesses, such as a local furniture-maker working in a garage workshop or a garment worker sewing in the kitchen. People who worked in "clerical" jobs had no choice but to work in an office as computers were too expensive. Today, technology has created more choice. By the 1990s, most people had computers and the Internet at home. By 2005, there were more mobile phones in UK than there were people. People found it much easier to work from home, and some employers offered their workers the chance to do so.

▲ Inventions such as mobile phones have made it much easier for people to work from home.

▲ A "wireless hotspot" logo in a British airport. This allows laptop users to use the Internet.

## ON THE MOVE

Travelling on business used to put workers out of touch with the office while they were on a plane. In 1988, telephones became available on Japanese airlines. Nowadays, most airlines provide in-seat telephones complete with ports for email and file transfer. Many hotels have special areas with Internet access via wireless connections. Some even have their own "business centres", equipped with the latest office technology.

> **66** *We have three separate work areas. One is a room of its own. My favourite is a desk in the living room that is its own space, but still feels part of the scene. Everything that I need, including a few hundred CDs, are within reach.* **99**
>
> Liz Strauss writes about working from home in the 21st century.

**THEN AND NOW**

Machines have also made a big difference to workers when they get home. Doing the laundry by hand used to take all day: a modern washing machine gives busy workers more time to relax at the end of the day. A microwave can create a hot meal in a few minutes.

## TIMELINE

**1958**
The silicon chip is invented.

**1969**
Arpanet (forerunner of the Internet) connects 4 computers in the United States.

**1981**
IBM launch their PC.

**1988**
There are 50,000 computers connected to Internet.

**1991**
The World Wide Web is first open to the public.

**1998**
There are 130 million web users worldwide.

**2005**
There are 1 billion web users in the world. About 42 per cent of UK homes have Internet access.

There are more mobile phones than people in Britain.

# WOMEN AND WORK

In the mid-1940s, the British government stopped the marriage bar, which forced female teachers and civil servants to stay single or resign in favour of male job seekers if they got married. In the 60 years since, life for working women has changed enormously.

## HOMEMAKER AND BREAD-WINNER

Before the war, women were usually taught that their main role in life was as homemakers. Most women thought that being a mother was their main career. Women were still told this after 1945, but the new Welfare State led to many new jobs that were filled by women, especially in nursing and teaching. In the 1950s and 60s, the economic boom led to thousands of new office and sales jobs which could be done on a part-time basis.

## WOMEN'S RIGHTS

In the 1970s, feminist movements, also known as Women's Liberation, demanded the same rights for women as men. This led to changes in the law, such as the 1970 Equal Pay Act, which said that women should be paid the same as men for the same work. Other new laws meant that bosses could not sack a woman just because she became pregnant. The other big change in the 1970s was that many more women were going to university. All these changes meant that by 2000, the number of women with jobs had grown to 70 per cent.

▲ A mother divides her attention up between her baby daughter and two young sons in 1950s London.

▶ A Women's Liberation parade in central London, (1972). The items of "oppression" are carried on a pole, including an apron, shopping bag, an item of washing and a silk stocking.

" *There was a saying that if you worked in the factory you were either among the needy or greedy. Most of us were needy.* "

Elizabeth Harrison describing attitudes to women factory workers in the early 1950s.

▲ A female account manager in an office in Leeds, 2005.

## TOUGH DECISIONS

Though women today are able to get better jobs, they are also expected to both work and bring up their children. Many firms are still not flexible and if a woman takes a couple of years off to have children it can be hard to get her career back on track.

Childcare can be expensive so in some cases women may feel it is not worth going back to work. As a result, it is especially hard for women to make it to the very top of their profession, to become company directors, senior surgeons or high court judges.

THEN AND NOW

The growth of women in work has partly been reflected in politics. In the 1950s, there were few women in politics. By 1979, Mrs Margaret Thatcher had become the first female prime minister. Yet in 2006, only 20 per cent of MPs were women.

## BUZZ BOX

Today there are more women in jobs traditionally seen as male. In 1961, just 3 per cent of the UK police force were women. By 2000, there were over 20,000 female police officers, making up 17 per cent of the police force. Female train drivers, fire officers and lawyers are all now increasingly common.

## TIMELINE

**1946**
The Marriage Bar is dropped from teaching and the Civil Service, allowing married women to work in those professions.

**1951**
Just 36 per cent of women are in the workforce.

**1970**
The Equal Pay Act is introduced.

**1971**
49 per cent of women are in the workforce.

**1975**
The Sex Discrimination Act and Employment Protection Act give further rights to working women.

**1993**
There are 12 million women at work in Britain, compared to 15 million men.

**2000**
Almost 70 per cent of women are in the workforce.

There has been a long history of immigrants coming to Britain to live and work. The British Nationality Act of 1948, however, gave all Commonwealth citizens the right to settle and work in Britain. Between 1951 and 2000, the number of ethnic minorities in Britain rose from 100,000 to over four million.

**BUZZ BOX**

Immigrants also created new businesses such as Indian and Chinese takeaways which are now popular across Britain. Indian food is a £3.2 billion industry in Britain.

### THE BOOM YEARS

After World War II, the UK was short of workers. Between 1945 and 1947, over 345,000 Europeans came to work in Britain, especially Italians and Poles. Then employers looked in other countries where they knew some English was spoken – especially the Commonwealth countries and colonies. In the 1950s, many immigrants were young men looking for work. Due to their lack of education and racial prejudice they were often forced to accept boring, poorly paid jobs. Other immigrants to Britain, such as nurses from the Caribbean and Ireland, brought with them valuable skills.

### SELF-EMPLOYMENT AND PREJUDICE

In the 1970s and 80s, thousands of immigrants in unskilled jobs, especially the textile and metal-working industries, lost their jobs. Many British Asians, especially Indians, became self-employed, running their own newspaper and grocery shops. Some operated larger enterprises such as clothing factories or wholesale warehouses.

By the 1990s, many of the British sons and daughters of immigrants were in higher education and becoming doctors, lawyers, engineers or business people. However, racial prejudice was still widespread and some professions were all but

▲ A group of immigrants work the land at a farm in Gloucestershire during the 1950s.

> 66 *I wanted to see the country that influenced my education... Most of us were just young men who came over on a wave of excitement to try life in a new country. There were a few older men who had worked in England during the war.* 99
>
> Dan Lawrence, who travelled on the ship *Empire Windrush* in 1948, which brought Jamaican immigrants to Britain.

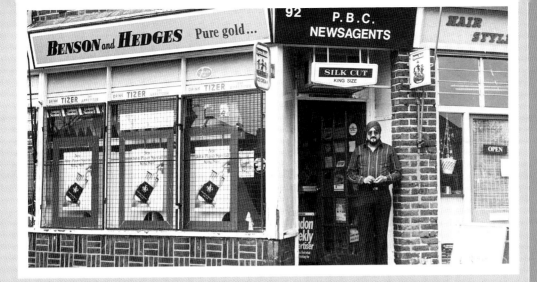

▲ An Asian corner shop from the 1980s.

closed to ethnic minorities. In 1997, not one of the 140 judges sitting in England's top courts belonged to an ethnic minority. The first non-white MPs since the war were elected in 1987. There were just 15 MPs from an ethnic minority elected at the 2005 General Election.

## THE NEW WAVE

In 2004, ten new countries joined the European Union (EU). They had the right to go and work in any other country in the EU. The largest of these newcomers was Poland. Between 2004 and 2007, over 500,000 Poles came to Britain to find work. Many found jobs in the service and building industry.

▼ Britain's richest man is an Asian – Indian steel tycoon, Lakshmi Mittal.

In the 1950s, there were many young Asians working in the northern textile mills. Following the decline of the textile industry in the 1970s and 80s, many turned to running their own small businesses. But since the 1990s the number of small shops run by Asians has gone done by 23 per cent, partly because so many young Asians are now going onto higher education.

## TIMELINE

**1948**
The British Nationality Act lets Commonwealth citizens live and work in Britain.

**1962**
The Commonwealth Immigration Act restricts immigration.

**1965**
The Race Relations Act outlaws racial discrimination.

**1971**
The Immigration Act makes it even harder for immigrants to enter Britain.

**1977**
The Commission for Racial Equality set up.

**2003**
The Race Directive strengthens the law on racial discrimination in the workplace.

**2006**
There are 300 Asian millionaires in Britain.

In the 1950s, many 14-year-olds went straight from school to full-time jobs. Today many young people go on to higher education. At the same time, older people are finding it hard to get jobs. This is partly because they expect higher wages, and some employers believe older workers are less flexible and willing to change than younger workers.

**THEN AND NOW**

Between 1945 and 1963, 2.5 million young men aged between 18 and 25 had to do 18 months of National Service in either the army, navy or air force. Only those working in coal mining, farming or the merchant navy were exempt. Today, there is little chance of the policy being reintroduced.

▲ University students relaxing in a student bar in London. The number of people in higher education has soared since the war.

## BUZZ BOX

In the past, it was very hard for people with disabilities to get jobs. However, more firms are realizing the benefits of employing people who are good workers but just happen to have a disability. Assistive technology – anything from touch screens to digital voice recorders – helps workers with disabilities to do tasks others take for granted.

## EDUCATION

In the past 50 years, the school leaving age has been raised repeatedly, and many more young people are going into higher education. Between the 1950s and the late 1990s, the number of young people aged 16 and over in full time education quadrupled. In the 1960s, most British men left school at 16 and went into low-skilled work. By 1999, 75 per cent of all young people from 16-18 were in education and training.

## YOUTH TRAINING SCHEMES

The 1980s saw the rise of government training schemes, such as the Youth Training Scheme (YTS), which aimed to give on-the-job training for 16-17 year olds. But some employers saw this as simply cheap labour. Many YTS workers received little training, especially in the kind of high technology skills required in the future. Today, YTS schemes have been replaced by vocational apprenticeships, where people learn "while they earn".

## THE ELDERLY

The last 50 years has seen a great rise in the numbers of elderly people, as we are living healthier and longer lives. However, many people are forced to retire when they want to carry on working. In October 2006, a new law came into force so that workers have the right to keep working if they want to after 65.

▼ An elderly mechanic at work.

▲ Young men learning how to garden on a YTS training scheme in Newcastle, 2001.

> " *Well – suddenly – you have no company any more. At work you've got other people, lots of company, a lot of chat. And you miss that terribly… You are alone and you just have to think of something to fill the day.* "

**A widowed nurse speaking of the shock of retirement in the late 1980s.**

## TIMELINE

**1908**
The Old Age Pension Act gives pensions to those over 70.

**1941**
Women are expected to live to 64 and men to 59.

**1954**
There are 122,000 students in higher education.

**1995**
Disability Discrimination Act gives rights to workers with disabilities.

**1997**
16 per cent of the population are aged 65 or over.

**2000**
There are 1,259,700 students in higher education.

**2006**
Changes in the law gives more rights to elderly workers.

In the 1950s and 60s, most people could find a job, though many women worked only in the home. During the 1970s, however, unemployment rose and has remained an issue ever since. Being unemployed can be very stressful and frustrating, especially when workers have families to support.

## FROM BOOM TO BUST

The government promised full employment after the war and thanks to the postwar boom this was achieved during the 1950s and 60s. In the 1970s, products made overseas were increasingly cheap due to higher wages in Britain. Many British factories closed down, and thousands became unemployed. The energy crises of 1973 and 1979 also led to job losses. Many coal mines shut down as homes switched to gas and electricity.

## STRIKES

To help British firms compete overseas, the government and industry tried to stop wages rising. The powerful trade unions fought back by striking. In 1974, the miners' strike caused the Labour government to lose power. During the 1979 "Winter of Discontent", there were widespread strikes as trade unions demanded higher pay rises. During the 1980s, unemployment rose even higher, reaching three million in 1982. In 1984, the miners went on strike again but had little success. New laws brought in by the Conservative Prime Minister Mrs Thatcher made it much harder to strike in the future. However, during the 1990s, unemployment fell steadily.

▲ Workers arrive for work at a power station in Sellafield during the 1950s. This period was a time of full employment, but by the 1970s this had ended.

THEN AND NOW

Trade Unions are organisations that help workers to fight for better pay and working conditions. In 1979, 13 million people were members of a union – more than half of all workers. Margaret Thatcher's Conservative governments weakened the powers of the unions in the 1980s, in particular by making it more difficult to strike. Despite a decline in numbers since the 1980s, there are still 7.3 million union members.

▲ The unemployed at a job centre in Wembley, 1985.

## LIFE ON THE DOLE

Since the creation of the Welfare State in 1948, the government has helped unemployed people with benefits. Labour exchanges (now called Job Centres) tried to help them find jobs. As long-term unemployment grew in the 1970s and 1980s, unemployed people became increasingly dependent on benefits. Since the 1990s, the government has introduced a variety of schemes to encourage unemployed people into work, such as training and advice. Although unemployment in Britain is higher than it was in the 1950s and 1960s, it is still the lowest of all the major industrialised countries.

> 66 *I had been made redundant before ... and I was confident I would be able to get another job. I've applied for several jobs a week in the five years I've been out of work and in that time I've had one interview. I've grown more and more disillusioned. It's like knocking on a friend's door and never getting an answer. It is a constant battle. I work harder while unemployed than when I was employed. There is endless form filling for little reward.* 99

An unemployed worker speaking in the 1990s.

▼ Striking miners confront a line of policemen in Nottingham during 1984.

BSE Short for Bovine Spongiform Encephalopathy, nicknamed Mad Cow Disease, a nervous disease that some scientists think can be caught by humans.

Depression A long-term fall in the economy, often accompanied by high employment and low economic growth.

Commonwealth An association of the UK and its former colonies such as India, Pakistan, Jamaica and Kenya.

EC (European Community), EU (European Union), EEC (European Economic Community) In 1958, the European Economic Community was created by the Treaty of Rome. As it grew and changed, the name changed too. It has also been known as the Common Market and the European Union. It is now known as the European Community.

Economy The business and work done by a community or country to make money.

Ethnic minority A person or group of people who have a different culture, religion or language to the main one in the place or country they live.

IT Information technology such as computers and the Internet.

Manufacturing Turning raw materials, such as steel, into finished products, such as bicycles.

Nationalize Turning private companies into ones run by the government. The opposite is to privatize, to make state-owned organisations into private companies.

National Service Between 1945 and 1963, young men aged from 18-26 years old had to do 18 months in the Armed Forces.

Rations A fixed allowance of food.

Sex discrimination When women are not paid or treated the same as men for doing the same job.

Self-employed People who work for themselves.

Strike When a group refuses to work in protest against low pay or bad work conditions.

Unemployed People who are out of work.

Trade Union An organisation that campaigns on behalf of worker for better pay or working conditions.

Welfare State A set of government programmes funded by taxes that provide free health, education, pensions and support for those who need it.

White-collar workers Office workers and professionals such as doctors and lawyers.

Blue-collar workers work in manufacturing. or work with their hands.

## Websites

http://www.britishpathe.com/
Download digital clips from the British Pathe Film Archive which covers news, sport, social history and entertainment from 1896 to 1970.

http://www.ukagriculture.com/countryside/countryside.cfm
The history of agriculture in Britain over the last 6,000 years.

http://www.homeworkelephant.co.uk/history-br.shtml
Materials on British history including Education, Trade Unions and famous businesspeople.

http://www.ncm.org.uk/
Website for the National Coal Mining Museum for England.

http://www.tuc.org.uk/tuc/students_tuc.cfm
The website of the Trades Union Congress (TUC) with a short history of trade unions in Britain and many links to other websites with information on trade unions.

http://www.screenonline.org.uk/history/
Facts and online digital films about unemployment in Britain in the 20th century.

Note to parents and teachers: Every effort has been made by the Publishers to ensure that these websites are suitable for children, that they are of the highest educational value, and that they contain no inappropriate or offensive material. However, because of the nature of the Internet, it is impossible to guarantee that the contents of these sites will not be altered. We strongly advise that Internet access is supervised by a responsible adult.

# Explorers

TURRIFF ACADEMY
LIBRARY

Peggy Burns

WAYLAND

# FAMOUS LIVES

## Kings and Queens
## Saints
## Inventors
## Explorers
## Artists
## Engineers

Cover pictures: (clockwise from left) Marco Polo, James Cook, Christopher Columbus

Editor: Joanna Bentley
Designer: Joyce Chester
Consultant: Norah Granger

First published in 1996 by Wayland (Publishers) Limited,
61 Western Road, Hove, East Sussex, BN3 1JD

**British Library Cataloguing in Publication Data**
Burns, Peggy 1941–
    Explorers. – (Famous Lives)
    1. Explorers – Biography – Juvenile literature
    2. Discoveries in geography – Juvenile literature
    I. Title
    910.9'22
ISBN 0 7502 1853 3

Typeset by Joyce Chester
Printed and bound by L.E.G.O. S.p.A., Vicenza, Italy

**Picture Acknowledgements**
The publishers wish to thank the following for allowing their pictures to be used in this book: AKG, London *front cover* (left and bottom right), *title page*, 5, 10, 11 (both), 13; Bridgeman Art Library, London/National Library of Australia, Canberra *front cover* (top right) and 16; Mary Evans Picture Library 4, 9, 14, 17 (top), 23, 27; Hulton Deutsch Collection Ltd 7 (top), 8, 18, 25; Ann Ronan at Image Select 15, 19; Topham Picturepoint 21; Visual Arts Library 6, 7 (bottom), 12; Wayland Picture Library *cover* (background), 17 (left), 20, 24.

# Contents

# *Marco Polo*

When Marco Polo was a small boy, he saw very little of his father, Nicolo. Nicolo Polo was often away from home.

When Marco was 17 years old he went with his father and uncle on a visit to China.

△ *Marco Polo leaves Venice to travel to China.*

China was thousands of kilometres from Venice, where the Polo family lived.

They crossed burning deserts and travelled through ice-cold mountains. They had many exciting adventures on the journey, and saw lots of strange things.

While they were in Russia they saw a fountain of oil gush out of the ground. In the desert, they were attacked by thieves. They crossed a sea of crispy salt as white as snow.

The long journey took three years.

△ *Marco Polo travelled by ship for much of his long journey.*

## DATES

Around **1254** Marco Polo born
**1271** Polo sets out for China
**1324** Death of Marco Polo

*An illustration from Polo's book showing the Chinese ruler Kublai Khan.*

When they arrived in China the Polo family was welcomed by the ruler, Kublai Khan. Marco quickly learned Chinese, and was given an important job. He became one of the Khan's most trusted servants.

After almost 17 years in China, Marco decided to go home. Back in Venice, Marco found that he had spent so many years travelling that he could not settle down.

He sailed off to fight in a war against the city of Genoa. But Marco was caught and put in prison.

Here he told a friend all about his years in China. He told of Kublai Khan's beautiful palaces, more splendid than any in Europe. He described the animals and birds of China. Many of them were not known in Europe.

The man wrote all the stories down. Years after Marco's death, in the year 1477, the stories were printed in a book.

The stories of Marco Polo's travels amazed everyone who read them.

△ *Marco Polo tells a fellow prisoner about his life in China.*

▽ *A picture from Marco Polo's stories about China.*

# Christopher Columbus

Christopher Columbus first left his home in Italy to go to sea when he was only 14. He listened as sailors told stories about the gold and precious stones that could be found in far-away lands. He grew up longing to sail away and explore these wonderful countries for himself.

Columbus dreamed of finding a new way to India and China. On the way he hoped to discover new lands full of treasure.

△ *Christopher Columbus persuades the King and Queen of Spain to pay for his voyage to discover new lands.*

In 1492 he sailed from Spain with three ships.

At first the voyage went well. But when they had been at sea for six weeks, the wind dropped. The sails hung limply down. Thick green seaweed gathered around the drifting ships.

For more than a week they drifted. The sailors were scared. They thought they would be stuck in the horrible weed for ever. A lot of them blamed Columbus. Some wanted to throw him over the side of the ship!

At last the wind blew. They came in sight of land. But where were they?

▽ *Columbus's fleet at sea.*

No Europeans had been to this land before. The only maps Columbus had were wrong. At that time, nobody knew that America existed.

Columbus believed they had sailed around the world and reached islands near Japan. He called the islands where they landed the West Indies.

But there was little gold there, and Columbus sailed on. Wherever they landed, the native Caribbean people were helpful, but Columbus found no treasure.

△ *Columbus lands in the West Indies in 1492.*

◁ *When he returned to Spain, Columbus thought he was close to finding a route to China.*

He went back to Spain, with a little gold and a few Caribbean people.

Columbus went back to the West Indies twice more, but he never found the riches he was searching for. When he died in 1506 he was a poor man.

*Columbus never found the route he thought there was to China.* ▽

## DATES

**1451** Birth of Christopher Columbus
**1492** Columbus sets out on his voyage of discovery
**1506** Death of Columbus

# Ferdinand Magellan

In 1519 many countries and seas had still not
been discovered by Europeans. Nobody had
sailed all around the world. Ferdinand Magellan,
a sea captain, decided to try. The King of Spain
gave him five ships and men to sail them.

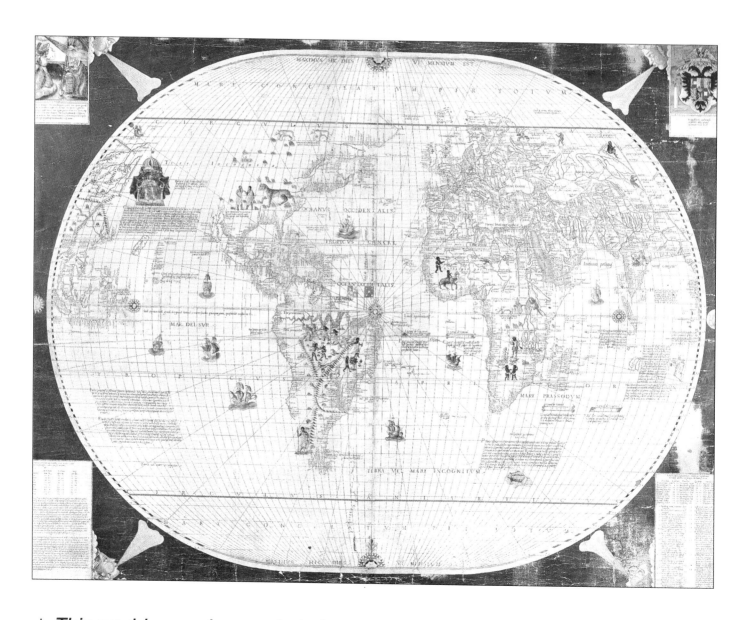

△ *This world map shows what places were known in Magellan's time.*

*Magellan's ship, the* Victoria, *sailing towards South America.* ▽

They sailed across the Atlantic and down the coast of South America. There were terrible storms, but Magellan would not turn back.

He was searching for a way round the southern tip of America, from the Atlantic to what was then called the Great South Sea. He explored every river mouth, hoping to find the passage.

One day they sailed around a point of land. In front of them lay the passage they were looking for. Storms still battered the ships. One of them sank. Giant waves swept men into the sea.

But Magellan turned his ships into the passage. White men had never been here before. Unknown land lay on both sides.

One month later they reached open sea. They were through! They were about to sail into the Great South Sea. The passage they sailed through is now called the Strait of Magellan.

Magellan gave the sea a new name. *'May the ocean be always as calm … as it is today,'* he said. *'In this hope I name it the Pacific Ocean.'*

They sailed on into the lonely Pacific, under a hot sun. The heat turned their food bad. The meat crawled with long white maggots. The water smelled so bad, they had to hold their noses as they drank. Some of the men became ill with hunger and scurvy. Soon they began to die.

△ *Sailing through the Strait of Magellan was a dangerous journey.*

## DATES

**1480** Ferdinand Magellan born

**1520** Magellan discovers and sails through the passage later named the Strait of Magellan

**1521** Magellan killed by natives in the Philippines

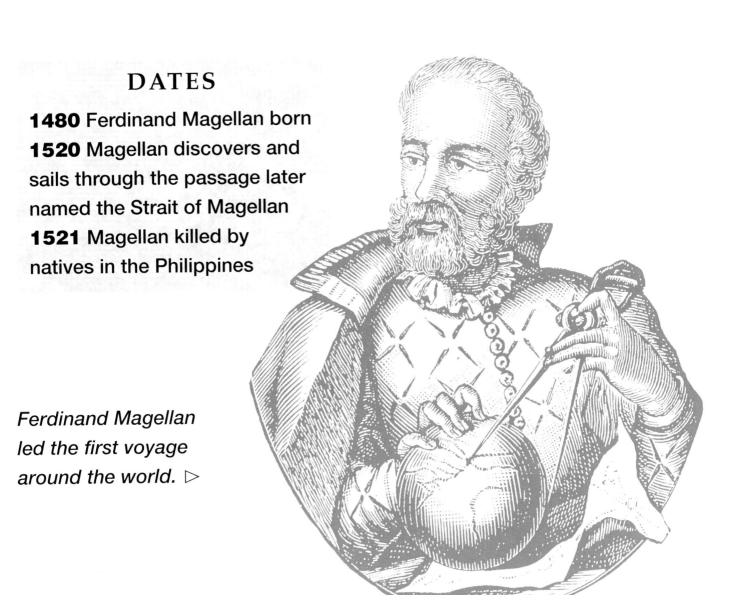

*Ferdinand Magellan led the first voyage around the world.* ▷

At last they saw an island. There was food and fresh water. They were saved!

In March 1521 they reached the Philippine Islands. Magellan had discovered and crossed the world's biggest ocean.

Only one ship and 19 men returned to Spain. Magellan himself was killed in the Philippines. But he had made history. He was the first explorer to sail around the world.

# James Cook

James Cook, a captain in the British Royal Navy, was very good at making maps of new countries.

In the year 1768 explorers had not yet discovered all the countries of the world.

Some people believed that there was a huge new country to the south of Australia. They named it *Terra Australis.*

Captain Cook was given the job of looking for *Terra Australis*. He was asked to find the new country, draw a map of it, and discover new plants and animals.

## DATES

**1728** James Cook born
**1768** Captain Cook sails in search of *Terra Australis*
**1779** Captain Cook killed by natives in the Hawaiian islands

◁ *Captain Cook.*

In 1768 Cook sailed from England in his ship, the *Endeavour.* After a year at sea they caught sight of a land they had never seen before. Captain Cook was thrilled. He thought he had found the new country.

Watched from the trees by some of the native people of this country, Cook took a few men ashore. But the men who had watched them were armed with wooden clubs and tried to capture Cook's boat.

△ *The* Endeavour *carried Captain Cook and his crew to New Zealand.*

Cook tried to show them that he meant them no harm. But there was a fight, and some of the native people were killed.

Cook sailed on up the coast, drawing maps of the new country as he went. But by now he realized that the land he had found was too small to be the imagined country *Terra Australis*.

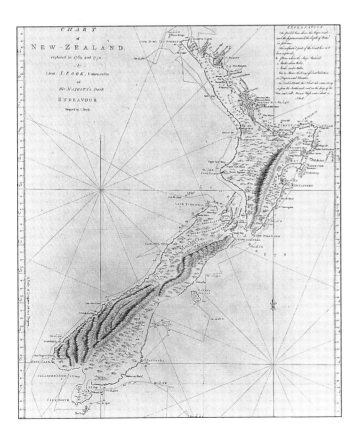

△ *This is the map based on Cook's chart of New Zealand.*

The country Captain Cook had found was actually New Zealand.

By this time the *Endeavour* had been at sea for two years. It was time to go home.

East of Australia the *Endeavour* ran on to huge spears of sharp coral at the Great Barrier Reef and stuck fast. Water poured in through a huge hole in the front of the ship!

It took many hours of hard work before Cook and his men could free the ship from the reef. They headed for the shore. They mended the hole and pumped out the water.

When Cook reached England in 1771, he had been at sea for three years. He had not found *Terra Australis*.

*When the* Endeavour *hit the coral reef she had to be repaired before Cook could head for home.* ▽

A year later, Cook was sent back to search once more. This time, he proved that there was no such country.

△ *Captain James Cook was killed on a later voyage to explore the Hawaiian islands in 1779.*

Captain James Cook's important discoveries made it possible to make a much better map of the world.

# Mary Kingsley

A hundred years ago most Europeans thought Africans were simple savages. They believed that African people should live more like Europeans. They taught them to read and write, wear clothes, and change the way they lived.

Mary Kingsley, who was very interested in Africa, did not agree. She thought that Europeans should let Africans live how they wanted.

Much of Africa was still not known to Europeans then. Mary decided to explore an unknown part of West Africa.

◁ *In Mary Kingsley's time women were not expected to want to explore unknown parts of Africa.*

The Fang tribe, who lived there, were cannibals. They sometimes killed and ate other people. Mary's friends were afraid she would be eaten and tried to stop her.

Before exploring Fang country, Mary spent a few months studying African life. Then, dressed in a long black skirt, with a pair of her brother's trousers underneath, she bravely set out.

When they first saw the Fang people, Mary and her guides held out their empty hands to show they had no weapons.

△ *Mary Kingsley travelled by canoe along the River Ogowe with a party of native guides.*

The Fang people crowded round Mary, but they did not hurt her. They had never seen a white person before.

Mary and her party went from village to village, spending time with the fierce Fang people.

One night, Mary found a bag in the hut where she was sleeping. The bag smelled terrible. Inside it, Mary found human ears, eyes and toes!

## DATES

**1862** Mary Kingsley born
**1895** Mary Kingsley visits the cannibal Fang tribe in West Africa
**1900** Death of Mary Kingsley

*Mary Kingsley returned to England knowing a great deal about Africa, its people and animals.* ▷

Mary Kingsley travelled 112 kilometres into unknown cannibal country. When she returned home, she wrote a book about her travels.

She had not been killed and eaten, as her friends had expected. Instead she had made friends with the fierce Fang tribe. They were, after all, only people with a different way of life.

◁ *People still use canoes to travel along the River Ogowe today.*

# Roald Amundsen

By 1900 explorers had been to almost every country in the world. Only two places had not been explored. These were the frozen lands of snow and ice – the North Pole in the Arctic and the South Pole in the Antarctic.

△ *Roald Amundsen was determined to be the first person to reach the South Pole.*

Roald Amundsen, who lived in Norway, wanted
to be first to reach one of these frozen lands.
A British explorer, Captain Scott, was already
planning to go to the Antarctic.

Amundsen decided to race him to the South Pole.

In January 1911 Amundsen reached Antarctica.
He was still 1,268 kilometres away from the Pole.

Amundsen worried all the time that Scott would get there before him.

In the freezing wind, ice and snow, Amundsen and his men set out for the South Pole. Teams of dogs pulled the sledges loaded with food and tents.

Soon the men had painful frostbite on their noses, toes and fingers. One of them wrote in his diary, *'The breath of men and dogs freezes the moment it hits the air'.*

*Amundsen's team put up the Norwegian flag at the South Pole.* ▽

*Roald Amundsen on
a later trip to the
North Pole.* ▷

They climbed upwards through snow-covered
mountains. Again and again they fell through
holes in the ice.

At last they were near the South Pole. They
wondered if Scott could have beaten them.
They reached the South Pole on 14 December
1911. There was no sign of Scott. Amundsen had
won the race. They had beaten Scott by 35 days.

27

# Timeline

| Year | Explorer | | How long ago? |
|------|----------|---|----------------|
| 1250 | |  | 750 years ago |
| 1254 | Marco Polo born in Venice | | |
| 1271 | Polo heads east with his father and uncle on a trading expedition | | |
| 1292 | Polo leaves China | | |
| 1295 | Polo arrives back in Venice | | |
| 1300 | | | 700 years ago |
| 1324 | Death of Marco Polo | | |
| 1350 | | | 650 years ago |
| 1400 | | | 600 years ago |
| 1450 | | | 550 years ago |
| 1451 | Christopher Columbus born | | |
| 1477 | Polo's book *Description of the World* printed | | |
| 1480 | Ferdinand Magellan born | | |
| 1492 | Columbus discovers the West Indies | | |
| 1500 | | | 500 years ago |
| 1506 | Death of Christopher Columbus | | |
| 1519 | Magellan sets out to sail around the world | | |
| 1521 | Magellan reaches the Philippines | | |
| 1521 | Magellan killed in the Philippines | 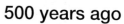 | |

| Year | Explorer | | How long ago? |
|------|----------|---|---------------|
| 1550 | | | 450 years ago |
| 1600 | | | 400 years ago |
| 1650 | | | 350 years ago |
| 1700 | | | 300 years ago |
| 1728 | James Cook born | | |
| 1746 | Cook first goes to sea | | |
| 1750 | | | 250 years ago |
| 1768 | Cook sails to search for *Terra Australis* | | |
| 1769–70 | Cook charts coast of New Zealand and east Australia | | |
| 1771 | Cook killed in Hawaii | | |
| 1800 | | | 200 years ago |
| 1850 | | | 150 years ago |
| 1862 | Mary Kingsley born | | |
| 1872 | Roald Amundsen born in Norway | | |
| 1893 | Kingsley first visits West Africa | | |
| 1895 | Kingsley explores unknown cannibal country | | |
| 1900 | Death of Mary Kingsley | | 100 years ago |
| 1910 | Amundsen begins his Antarctic expedition | | |
| 1911 | Amundsen reaches the South Pole | | |
| 1928 | Death of Amundsen | | |

# Words to look up

*Cannibals*  People who eat other people.

*Caribbean*  People who live on the islands around the Caribbean Sea.

*Coral*  Tiny animals that live closely together in the sea, forming a wall called a reef.

*Fleet*  A group of ships sailing together.

*Frostbite*  When freezing temperatures destroy exposed parts of the body, such as fingers and toes.

*Great Barrier Reef*  A 2,000 kilometre-long coral reef off the north-east coast of Australia. It is the largest coral reef in the world.

*Maggots*  The young form of insects, which can be found in food that is going bad.

*Native*  Born in a particular place.

*North Pole*  The furthest point north on Earth.

*Savages*  Wild, uncivilized people.

*Scurvy*  A disease caused by not eating enough food containing Vitamin C. Fruit such as oranges and lemons contains Vitamin C.

*South Pole*  The furthest point south on Earth.

# Other books to look at

*Captain Cook* by Alan Blackwood,
  Wayland, 1986.
*Columbus – The Triumphant Failure* by
  Oliver Postgate and Naomi Linnell,
Kingfisher Books, 1991.
*Follow the Dream – The Story of
  Christopher Columbus* by Peter Sis,
  Julia MacRae Books, 1992.

# Some places to see

**Barcelona**, Spain. Christopher
  Columbus's ship the *Santa Marie* is
  moored at Barcelona Docks.

**Captain Cook Birthplace
  Museum**, Middlesborough,
  Cleveland. This museum follows
  Captain Cook's life from his birth on
  its site to his death in Hawaii.

**Captain Cook's School Room**,
  Great Ayton, Middlesborough,
  Cleveland. Cook grew up in Great
  Ayton, and this museum contains
  many of his personal belongings,
  maps and charts.

# Index